IMAGES
of America

RED RIVER
STEAMBOATS

IMAGES
of America

RED RIVER
STEAMBOATS

Gary Joiner and Eric Brock

ARCADIA
PUBLISHING

Published by Arcadia Publishing
Charleston, South Carolina

Library of Congress Catalog Card Number: 99-63306

For all general information contact Arcadia Publishing at:
Telephone 843-853-2070
Fax 843-853-0044
E-Mail sales@arcadiapublishing.com
For customer service and orders:
Toll-Free 1-888-313-2665

Visit us on the Internet at www.arcadiapublishing.com

Dedicated to Cristina Walker and Marilyn Joiner

CONTENTS

From humble keelboats and flatboats to mighty steamboats, the craft that once plied the rivers of the South have become romantic symbols of the region, and of an age gone by. (*Engraving by John Wolcott Adams; Collection of the Authors*)

INTRODUCTION

The Red River is one of the major tributaries of the Mississippi, flowing from its source in New Mexico, into Texas where it forms the Texas-Oklahoma border. From there it continues through the southwest corner of Arkansas into Louisiana, diagonally crossing the state and finally emptying into the Mississippi at Avoylles Parish. In all, the Red flows some 1,300 miles, making it the eighth longest river in the continental U.S. and the tenth in all of North America. Another of the river's claims to fame is the silt it carries along its journey. In fact, it is one of the highest silt-load bearing rivers in the country and receives its name from the reddish color given its waters by the silt they carry.

In the 18th century the Red River was known by the French settlers as the *Fleuve Rouge*. It was then some 1,800 miles long, its shorter modern length coming from the artificial cutting of new channels across the short parts of its meanders, leaving it straighter, and creating oxbow lakes in the process. But the French were not the first to dwell along the river's banks. Archaeological evidence points to Native American habitation of the region for over 5,000 years. Some of the oldest human settlements in North America have been found in the area watered by the Red and Ouachita Rivers, just west of the Mississippi.

Spanish explorers reached the Red River in the 16th century, and discovered a massive jam of fallen trees and debris. This natural damming came to be known as "The Great Raft." The Caddo Indians indicated that the jam extended for a great distance and could not recall a time when it did not exist. It is now believed that the Raft extended some 400 miles upstream from modern Natchitoches. Natchitoches, founded in 1714, and the oldest city not only in Louisiana but in all the vast area of the Louisiana Purchase, owes its very existence to the Raft. Because of it, sites upstream were not accessible and so the initial French base of operations in Louisiana was set up at the Raft's end.

Although the French and Spanish explored the region during the 18th century, a thorough effort to explore and document the river did not occur until it came into the hands of the United States in 1803. The first thorough exploration occurred in 1806 with the Freeman-Custis Expedition, which ascended the Red, but was eventually stopped by Spanish military forces.

In 1814, Capt. Henry Miller Shreve entered the Red River chronicle, forever changing its destiny. In December of that year Shreve took the first steamboat up the Red, as far as the rapids above Alexandria. The vessel, the *Enterprise*, a year later became the first steamboat to successfully negotiate the rapids and reach Natchitoches. By 1830, steamboats had penetrated another hundred river-miles northward to the foot of the Great Raft, just below the site of modern Shreveport.

Shreve's name has been fittingly preserved in the naming of the city of Shreveport in his honor. In 1833, Shreve, commanding the U.S. Army Corps of Engineers on the Red, began the Herculean task of breaking up the Great Raft. Opening the length of the Red River to navigation meant opening one of the great water highways of North America to traffic, connecting the vast area drained by the Red to the Mississippi. Connecting the Red River's watershed to the great markets of New Orleans via the Mississippi made the area attractive for settlers and agriculture. Opening the Red also created a river corridor into Mexico, for Texas was then part of that nation. Indeed, when founded in 1836, Shreveport was the westernmost town in the United States.

Captain Shreve invented the snagboat, a double-hulled craft with a large crane mounted between the hulls. Using this device the "snags" (large debris such as tree trunks clogging the river) could be hauled aboard, cut up, then flung to shore to be burned or to decay. Clearing the Raft in such a manner was an arduous task, but Shreve was up to the job. His skills as an engineer and inventor, and his crucial role in clearing the Great Raft, helped build commerce along the rivers of the South, West, and Midwest. Shreve was one of the most important figures who paved the way for the westward expansion of the United States.

Ironically, Henry Shreve never lived in the city that bears his name, nor did he see the completion of the clearing of the Great Raft. He died in St. Louis in 1851. Traffic to and from Shreveport and into the bayous, swamps, and lakes of Northwest Louisiana and East Texas was common during his lifetime, however. Nevertheless, the Great Raft was not completely obliterated until 1874.

During the Civil War, gunboats and other warships plied the Red as Union forces pushed forward toward Shreveport, then the Confederate capital of Louisiana. The Union naval presence was formidable, but it was met by the ingenuity of Confederate river defenses and a much smaller Confederate fleet. Although conflicts occurred on the river's waters, it was the events occurring on land that ultimately turned the Union ships back, ensuring that Shreveport would not fall into Federal hands, as cities downstream had done. In their retreat, the Union forces burned much in their path, including plantations along the river's bank, and the entire city of Alexandria.

After the war, commerce resumed on the Red, but a litany of disasters led to the river being dubbed a "steamboat graveyard." One of the worst disasters occurred on June 9, 1865, when the overloaded troop ship *Kentucky* struck a snag and burned just below Shreveport. Over 100 soldiers and as many as 900 civilians perished in the wreck. In February 1869, the river steamer *Mittie Stephens* sank in flames on Caddo Lake en route from Shreveport to Jefferson, Texas, also with considerable loss of life. These are the most famous steamboat wrecks on the Red and its tributaries, but they are by no means the only ones. Both were the subjects of archaeological studies during the 1990s. Many others have yet to be explored.

Despite numerous disasters, regular navigation on the Red River continued for over a century. Huge craft loaded with North Louisiana cotton plied the river between Shreveport and New Orleans. Packet steamers carried mail and passengers to dozens of stops along the river's length. Showboats brought entertainment to the towns and cities along the banks of the Red, as well. By the start of the 20th century, however, the railroad was replacing the steamboat as the primary source of transportation in the South. By the era of the First World War, steamboat service as far north as Shreveport had virtually ceased. By the 1930s, steamboats had vanished from the Red altogether and the river quickly silted up, in time becoming unnavigable once again. In the mid-20th century, proposals to re-open the Red to navigation began to be seriously pondered, but nothing came of them until the 1980s, when the first steps toward the reclamation of the Red as a navigable waterway were taken. The ongoing process of opening the Red River to navigation continues to this day. Once again, barges can be seen on the river, as well as several floating casinos built to approximate the appearance of steamboats of old. Now, as in the beginning, credit for the actual opening of the Red River goes to the U.S. Army Corps of Engineers. The legacy of Henry Miller Shreve lives on.

This book is a pictorial history of navigation on the Red River. It offers views spanning the Great Raft, the opening of the river to navigation and commerce, the Civil War on the Red River, and the twilight of commercial steam navigation on the Red. Many craft that once traveled the Red River were never photographed. Some came and went before the dawn of photography itself. A few of these were illustrated in engravings, but illustrations of numerous early boats simply do not exist. We are fortunate that many vessels were photographed and that those photographs provide us with a wealth of significant images of the rich heritage of the age of steam on the Red River.

The pictures illustrating this book are drawn from numerous sources, and many of them have never before been published. The authors hope this volume will add to the knowledge of the steamboats that once ran on the Red River, its tributaries and associated waterways. They also hope that it will reflect positively on the people who operated those craft; in doing so, they helped to shape the history of the American South and the nation's great expansion westward.

One

THE GREAT RAFT
AND THE OPENING
OF THE RED RIVER

The Great Raft stretched for more than 400 miles, clogging the river from bank to bank, and making navigation on its waters impossible. At some points, the thickness of the congestion was so great that a person could cross on horseback without getting either horse or rider the least bit damp. (*LSU-Shreveport Noel Library Archives*)

These are two views of the Great Raft above Shreveport, made in 1873 by either R.B. Talfor or George Woodruff, both of whom photographed the Raft for the Army Corps of Engineers. No photographic views of the Raft were made during Captain Shreve's lifetime, but the portion of the Raft shown here appears no different than when Shreve first laid eyes upon it. *(Both photos: LSU-Shreveport Noel Library Archives)*

Here are two further views of the river made during the clearing of the Great Raft north of Shreveport in 1873 and 1874. Again, the scene was unchanged from that experienced by Shreve and his engineers 40 years earlier, and a few miles to the south. *(Both photos: LSU-Shreveport Noel Library Archives)*

Capt. Henry Miller Shreve (1785–1851) was a native of New Jersey. The son of a Quaker family, he was raised in Pennsylvania and later resided in Kentucky and Missouri. His pioneering work in opening the rivers of the American South and Midwest to commerce earned him a prominent place in American history. His work in initiating the removal of the Great Raft, thereby opening the Red River and the lands it drained to settlement, caused the city of Shreveport, Louisiana, to be named in his honor. *(Authors)*

Pictured here are two of Captain Shreve's first steamboats. At top is the *George Washington*, built by Shreve in 1824, which ran principally on the Mississippi River. Below is its less fortunate predecessor, the *Washington*, which exploded on June 16, 1816, on the Mississippi. It was the first steamboat explosion on the western waters. Eight were killed, but the boat was rebuilt. (*Both Illustrations: Authors*)

Shreve was an innovator, carrying steamboat design to new levels during the early decades of steam navigation. He was also an important inventor in his own right. His most significant invention combined his steamboat innovations with his engineering skills. The double-hulled snagboat allowed for the clearing of the Great Raft on the Red River and made possible the maintenance of America's navigable waterways thereafter. Shown is a model of Shreve's 1837 snagboat *Archimedes*, which was used in clearing the Raft. (*Goodloe R. Stuck*)

Though Captain Shreve owned property in Shreveport (first called Shreve Town when founded in 1836 and renamed in 1839), he never lived there. When he retired, it was to St. Louis, Missouri. There he died on March 6, 1851, at the age of 65. He is buried with his wife and children at Bellefontaine Cemetery, overlooking the Mississippi. (*Authors*)

14

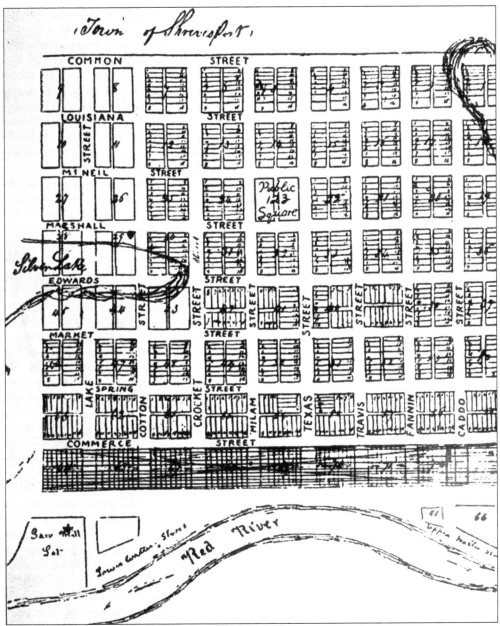

The original plan of the town of Shreveport provided for eight streets to run north to south, and eight from east to west. Streets were named by Shreve himself, several in honor of the heroes of the Texas Revolution, then taking place nearby. On this map, the top is west. The Red River flows along the east side of town at bottom. The crossed-out blocks were never laid out; their area, instead, became the wide wharf known as "the Levee." Today the area shown is Shreveport's central business district. (*Authors*)

Shown here is a rare image of flatboats of the sort once common on the Red River. These were the earliest commercial craft to ply the river. Departing for the New Orleans markets downstream, the flatboats simply floated with the current. Upon reaching their destination, they were broken up and sold for lumber. *(LSU-Shreveport Noel Library Archives)*

The riverfront at Shreveport appears much the same in this 1873 image as it had for the city's previous 37 years. Much of the time, steamboats could be seen moored along the Commerce Street "levee." However, none are present in this image by Lt. Eugene A. Woodruff of the Army Corps of Engineers, then working to clear the Great Raft north of town. *(Authors)*

The Army Corps' snagboat, *Aid,* is seen here on one of the bayous adjacent to the Red River above Shreveport. The effort to clear the Great Raft from the Red also involved opening various tributaries to traffic. *(Authors)*

This is an exceptional engraving of a snagboat in action. Although the background terrain clearly indicates that this view is not on the Red River, the style of boat and the method of removing obstacles from the water is identical to those used in opening the Red to navigation. The double hull can clearly be seen as a huge log is hauled aboard to be cut up. (*Harper's Weekly*)

Lt. Eugene A. Woodruff (right), an officer of the Army Corps of Engineers, was a successor to Captain Shreve in directing efforts to clear the Great Raft. He opened much of the river above Shreveport before succumbing to yellow fever in September 1873 at the age of 31. His brother, Lt. George S. Woodruff (below), succeeded him and directed the final elimination of the Great Raft. George Woodruff died in Iowa in the 1930s. Eugene is buried in Shreveport's Oakland Cemetery. (*Both photos: Authors*)

Shown are two views of the snagboat, *Aid,* on the Red River during the final removal of the Great Raft in 1873. The *Aid* was built in Pittsburgh, Pennsylvania, in 1869 and was initially designed to raise sunken steamboats clogging the Ohio and Mississippi Rivers. It arrived in Shreveport in January 1873 to begin the final assault on the remnants of the Great Raft. *(Both photos: Authors)*

In addition to snagboats, the Corps of Engineers crew used steam saws mounted on flatboats to facilitate the clearing of debris, as seen in this photograph by R.B. Talfor. Sometimes, nitroglycerin was used to blast embedded debris out of place. (*LSU-Shreveport Noel Library Archives*)

On May 16, 1873, R.B. Talfor photographed the *R.T. Bryarly* as she passed through the channel opened by Lt. Eugene Woodruff's crew. The *R.T. Bryarly*, on that day, became the first steamboat to enter the upper reaches of the Red River unhindered by the Great Raft at any point. For the next several months, until April 1874, the Corps of Engineers continued to work to ensure that the Raft would not re-form. The passage up the river by the *R.T. Bryarly*, however, signaled that the work begun by Captain Shreve in 1833 had been successfully completed. The *R.T. Bryarly* sank at Pecan Point on the Red River on September 19, 1876. *(LSU-Shreveport Noel Library Archives)*

Above: A small snagboat of Woodruff's crew, is photographed on the Red River above Shreveport in the spring of 1873. *Below*: The government snagboat *E.A. Woodruff*, named in memory of Lt. Eugene Augustus Woodruff, is seen on the Ohio River. Built in 1874, the *E.A. Woodruff* remained a working vessel until 1940. *(Top: LSU-Shreveport Noel Library Archives; Bottom: Roland J. Achee)*

Two important early steamboats that ran on the Red River were the *Car of Commerce*, which ran principally on the Ohio in the 1840s but is documented to have also been on the Mississippi and Red Rivers, and the *Mittie Stephens*, which ran on the Red and Mississippi Rivers in the 1860s. The *Car of Commerce* is seen above at Cincinnati in 1848. The *Mittie Stephens* is seen below in a model. Both boats were wrecked. The *Car of Commerce* foundered near Louisville, Kentucky in December 1848, with no injuries. The *Mittie Stephens* burned and sank on Caddo Lake near Jefferson, Texas, on February 11, 1869, with the loss of 56 passengers and crew. (*Top: Cincinnati & Hamilton County Library; Bottom: Jesse DeWare IV.*)

Passengers wait for a sidewheel steamboat in a scene typical of travel on the Red River in the middle part of the 19th century. From the 1840s through the end of the century, steamboats provided the fastest, safest, and most comfortable means of transportation available to Southern travelers. (*Every Saturday*)

The steamboat *Princess*, above, built in 1855, set records for speed. On February 27, 1859, she exploded near Baton Rouge with the loss of 70 lives. Prior to that, the *Princess* ran on the Mississippi between New Orleans and Vicksburg and on the Red between Shreveport and New Orleans. The *Era No. 2*, seen here loaded with Shreveport cotton, bound for New Orleans in 1859, was owned by the Kouns Line of Shreveport. Between 1856 and 1892, thirteen boats named *Era* operated on the Red and Mississippi Rivers. In 1861, *Era No. 2* was converted into a tinclad gunboat. She sank on the Red River May 6, 1864. (*Top: LSU-Shreveport Noel Library Archives; Bottom: Authors*)

The *Belle Creole,* above, an important steamboat of the Mississippi, Ohio, Arkansas, and Red River trade, is seen in this view in port at Cincinnati. In 1861, she sank on the Mississippi but was raised, rebuilt, and outfitted as a U.S. transport boat, serving with Admiral Porter on the Red River. She burned at New Orleans, May 28, 1864. The importance of steamboats to the Louisiana economy is evident from the vignette on the $1 State of Louisiana banknote (below) issued at Shreveport, which was the state capital in 1864. A female figure representing "Abundance" stands at left. Agriculture and steamboat transportation were integral to the success of the state's 19th-century economy.

Pictured above is the steamer transporting Dan Rice's Circus in 1860. Rice performed throughout the South and was one of the most popular entertainers of his day. Unlike the showboats of the era, which were typically barges pushed or pulled by small steam-powered tugboats, Rice's troupe used a full-sized, specially-equipped steamboat, performing under tents on shore. Shown below is the *Laurel Hill,* built in 1859. It was very nearly a twin to the ill-fated *Mittie Stephens.* Both were later used as transports with Admiral Porter's fleet on the Red during the Civil War. (*Top: Authors; Bottom: LSU-Shreveport Noel Library Archives*)

A busy day at the riverfront during the period preceding the Civil War would have looked like this. The packet boats that ran from Shreveport to New Orleans, stopping at points in-between, are seen loading and off-loading their cargoes. The wharf was a busy place with passengers, workmen, cotton factors, brokers, dealers, and planters all present during peak hours. Business deals were transacted right on the riverbank and the sights, sounds, and smells of a busy marketplace were constantly present. (*Authors*)

Both the *Baltic* and the *Diana* operated on the Red River before the Civil War, though the famous race between them occurred on the Mississippi. On February 9, 1860, the two steamboats raced upstream, as seen in this painting by George F. Fuller. The *Baltic* won. During the Civil War, both boats were used by Admiral Porter as transports on the Red. Below is an 1859 view of Shreveport-New Orleans Red River packet boats docked at New Orleans. Among those in the photograph are the *Col. T.H. Judson, LeCompte, Milton Relf, Dr. Buffington, Starlight*, and *Messenger. (Both photos: LSU-Shreveport Noel Library Archives)*

The Kouns Line's Shreveport-New Orleans express mail packet, *Grey Eagle* (pictured above), was built in 1860 and was in operation into 1869. Built in 1860, she was used by the Confederacy to transport guns during the Civil War. She was sold and dismantled in 1869, her machinery going to another boat, the *Grand Era*. The re-use of machinery and salvageable parts of steamboats was common practice throughout the steamboat era. (*LSU-Shreveport Noel Library Archives*)

Pictured here are three Red River packets at New Orleans. The vessel on the right is the *Jesse K. Bell*, later seized by the Union Army at Louisville in 1861 and used by Gen. Lew Wallace as his headquarters during the Tennessee Campaign. She burned at St. Louis, September 13, 1863. A second *Jesse K. Bell* was built by the Red River Line in 1879 and dismantled in 1897. Both were named for the president of the New Orleans National Bank. (*Authors*)

Two

THE CIVIL WAR ON THE RED RIVER

In February 1864, a massive Union fleet, commanded by Adm. David Dixon Porter, entered the Red River intent upon capturing the city of Shreveport. Shreveport was the Confederate capital of Louisiana and headquarters of the Trans-Mississippi Department of the Confederate Army. The Union had by then taken New Orleans and much of South Louisiana, and the advance of Porter's fleet, supported by Gen. Nathaniel P. Banks's land-based army, would bring the central part of the state into Union hands as well. Nevertheless, a decisive Confederate victory at Mansfield, Louisiana, turned the Federal troops and gunboats back, retreating before ever reaching Shreveport, which remained free and unscathed. *(Harper's Weekly)*

This image is of the Red River in 1864. It is the scene that met the Union fleet on Admiral Porter's Red River Expedition during the Red River Campaign. Confederate engineers, under Gen. William Boggs, successfully diverted the majority of the river's flow into Bayou Pierre via Tone's Bayou, just below Shreveport. Meanwhile, on land, Gen. Edmund Kirby Smith and Maj. Gen. Richard Taylor, despite clashes with one another over strategy, successfully led their troops in repelling a much larger foe—partly with the river's help. (*Authors*)

One of Admiral Porter's tinclad gunboats was the USS *Nymph*, which served in the Red River Campaign. Unlike ironclads, which were completely armored, tinclads had armor plating only on their main decks, while the upper "boiler deck" was completely vulnerable. (*Naval Historical Center*)

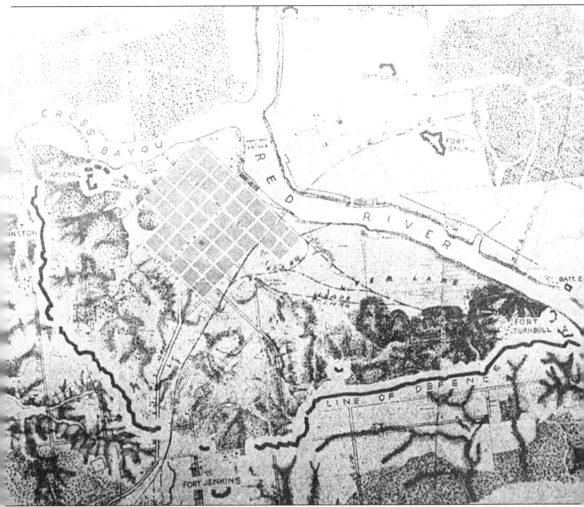

The Confederate defenses of Shreveport are shown on this 1864 map by Lieutenant Heilfrich, after a survey by C.U. Lenoir, under the direction of Maj. Richard Venable of the Confederate Corps of Engineers. Known as "The Venable Map," it shows the string of forts and batteries linking defensive earthworks surrounding the city. These earthworks were built largely by slaves pressed into service by Gen. Kirby Smith for that purpose in 1863. A lack of cannon led to the "arming" of some of the fortifications with charred logs to resemble cannon from a distance. The ruse was not necessary however, as the Federal forces never made it to Shreveport. (*Authors*)

Shreveport's Confederate Naval Yard produced the ironclad gunboat CSS *Missouri* and repaired and refitted the ironclad CSS *William H. Webb,* but perhaps the most remarkable—and least known—vessels built there were five experimental submarines. Each was 40 feet long, 40 inches wide, and 4 feet deep and could deliver contact mines to enemy vessels. The submarines were never utilized, however. One was sent to Houston and the other four were sunk in the Red River when the Trans-Mississippi Confederacy surrendered in June 1865. The photograph above depicts a similar, though smaller, Confederate submarine found in Lake Pontchartrain in 1878. Long believed to be the *Pioneer,* it is now known not to have been. Its origin is a mystery. The photograph was made by G.F. Mugnier at Spanish Fort, New Orleans, in 1890. *(Authors)*

At the opposite end of the Red River from Shreveport, close to the river's mouth in Avoylles Parish, Louisiana, stood Fort DeRussy, ordered built by Gen. E. Kirby Smith. On March 12, 1864, the fort was taken by Union troops, opening the Red to the Federal naval advance towards Shreveport. *(Frank Leslie's Illustrated News)*

Between the mouth of the Red and Shreveport lay Alexandria, Louisiana, an important city located just below the rapids. The Union fleet under Admiral Porter reached Alexandria on March 16, 1864, taking the city peacefully. Meanwhile Maj. Gen. Richard Taylor's troops had evacuated the city. Many civilian refugees, too, had left for Shreveport, and all public property had been loaded on steamboats bound for the capital, leaving little for the Union to seize. *(Authors)*

Northwest of Alexandria lay the village of Grand Ecore. Its defensive earthworks are seen here. It was here that Union Maj. Gen. Nathaniel P. Banks, whose army was hitherto supported by Admiral Porter's fleet, decided to turn away from the river and advance toward Shreveport by an inland route. The decision proved to be a fateful mistake for the Union. Leaving the river behind at Grand Ecore, Banks headed north on April 6, 1864, as Porter moved north on the river. Separated, both would be turned back within days. *(LSU-Shreveport Noel Library Archives)*

Adm. David Dixon Porter, U.S. Navy, led the Union Naval advance toward Shreveport, which came to be known as the Red River Campaign. His large fleet provided back-up support for General Banks's army—until Banks's fatal decision to march north toward Shreveport along a path away from the river's safety. (*Naval Historical Center*)

An exceedingly rare and important view of Admiral Porter's fleet assembled on the Mississippi River at Memphis, just prior to its departure for the mouth of the Red River and for Shreveport, is shown here. The transports, ironclad gunboats, and tinclad gunboats seen in this image were all on the Red River within days of this photograph being made. (*Library of Congress*)

These are two views of the *Black Hawk*, Admiral Porter's flagship. Built as the *New Uncle Sam* in 1857, she was sold to the U.S. Navy in 1862. With Porter on the Red River throughout the Campaign, she did not last long after the war, sinking on the Mississippi near Mound City, Illinois, on April 22, 1865. *(Top: Library of Congress; Bottom: LSU-Shreveport Noel Library Archives)*

The *New Falls City* would play one of the most significant roles of any vessel involved in the saga of the Red River Campaign. Built at Paducah, Kentucky, in 1858, the *New Falls City* was an 880-ton "floating palace." In 1864, however, she was taken up the Red River by Confederate forces and purposely sunk across the river's breadth near Loggy Bayou, south of Shreveport. The wreck was described by Admiral Porter in a letter to General Sherman as "the smartest thing I ever knew the rebels to do." Attached to the portion of the steamer that jutted up above the water was a sign painted in large letters inviting the Yankees to "attend a ball in Shreveport." A Confederate victory at nearby Mansfield and a strategic victory at Pleasant Hill, however, forced Porter to abandon any effort at removing the sunken ship, turning his fleet around instead. The expected battle at Shreveport was thus averted. (*Howard-Tilton Library, Tulane University*)

Here are two views of the Union ironclad gunboat *Essex*, one of a dozen Union ironclads with Porter on the Red River. Built as the snagboat *New Era* in 1856, the *Essex* was converted into an ironclad in 1861. The *Essex* was on the Mississippi prior to the Red River Campaign and is one of the best-known ironclad gunboats of the Civil War. Following her service on the Red, she saw action at Fort Henry, where she exploded. In 1870, she was scrapped at Memphis. *(Top: Library of Congress; Bottom: Naval Historical Center)*

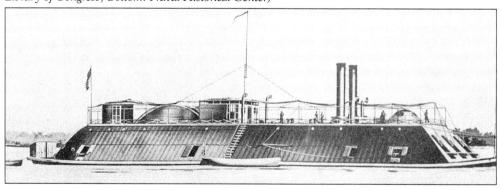

Above is another view of the USS *Essex*, here seen on the Mississippi River at Baton Rouge shortly before departing for the Red with Admiral Porter's Expedition. Below is the Union ironclad gunboat *Benton*. Built as the wrecking boat *Submarine No. 7* by the noted engineer James B. Eads, she was converted into an ironclad in 1861. With Porter on the Red River, she was sold for scrap after the war. (*Top: Naval Historical Center; Bottom: Library of Congress*)

This is a remarkable view of three of the seven River City-class ironclad gunboats that were part of Admiral Porter's fleet on the Red River. These were the *Carondelet, Chillicothe, Louisville, Mound City, Cairo, Cincinnati,* and *Pittsburg.* Specifically which three of the seven are shown cannot be stated with accuracy. (*Naval Historical Center*)

These are closer views of two River City-class ironclad gunboats such as was used by the Union during the Red River Campaign. The vessel shown above is the USS *Cincinnati*, which did not serve on the Red but which is identical in design to the five River City-class ironclads that did. The *Cincinnati* was sunk twice on the Mississippi during the course of the Civil War. Below is the *Pittsburg*, sister to the *Cincinnati*. She saw service with Porter on the Red River. *(Top: Naval Historical Center; Bottom: Library of Congress)*

Above is the only known photograph of the Union ironclad gunboat USS *Cairo*. Designed by Samuel M. Pook and known as a "Pook Turtle," the *Cairo* was built by the engineer James B. Eads at St. Louis. The *Cairo* was one of the most important of the Union ironclads in service on the Mississippi River between Louisiana and Mississippi during the first Federal attempts to open the Mississippi "unvexed," and to take the mouth of the Red. She was sunk by a Confederate mine on the Yazoo River in October 1862. In 1964, she was raised, and today is displayed at the Vicksburg National Military Park in Mississippi. (*Library of Congress*)

U.S.S. Choctaw Lieut Commande F.M. Ramsay.

The Union ironclad gunboats *Choctaw* (top) and *Lafayette* (below), are pictured here with Admiral Porter's fleet on the Red River. The ram *Choctaw* carried eight guns; the *Lafayette* carried ten. Both weighed in at 1,000 tons and had independent sidewheels. They were clad with sheet iron carried to a yard below the waterline. *(Both photos: Library of Congress)*

The ironclad gunboat USS *Eastport* was built in 1852. She was in the process of conversion into an ironclad by the Confederacy when captured by the Union Navy on the Tennessee River. The *Eastport* was the largest of the dozen ironclads with Porter during the Red River Expedition. Near Grand Ecore, she struck a Confederate mine and sank, creating a troublesome obstacle for the rest of the Union fleet behind her. (*Library of Congress*)

Commander S.L. Phelps, captain of the *Eastport*, was commander of the vessel under Admiral Porter during the Red River Expedition. When his ship sank, he led the effort to remove her so the rest of the Union fleet could pass on their way northward toward Shreveport. After days of constant toil, Phelps and the *Eastport* crew raised their stricken ship, floating her 40 miles downstream before it became evident her damage was irreparable. On April 26, 1864, the *Eastport* was blown up near Montgomery, in Grant Parish, Louisiana. Phelps is shown here late in life. (*Library of Congress*)

Another Union gunboat lost on the Red River was the tinclad *Covington*, which on May 5, 1864, was heavily damaged by shore batteries near the mouth of Dunn's Bayou—a tributary of the Red. To prevent her capture by Confederate forces, her crew blew her up. Although the written depiction of the incident in *Leslie's* was accurate, the engraving shown is a fanciful rendition. The *Covington* was, in fact, a tinclad gunboat, not an ironclad as portrayed. (*Frank Leslie's Illustrated News*)

Pictured here are two views of the Union ironclad gunboat *Neosho*, another of the 25 gunboats, 12 of which were ironclads, with Porter on the Red River. The 523-ton monitor class *Neosho* was designed and built by James B. Eads for the Union Navy at St. Louis in 1862. She carried four guns. (*Top: Naval Historical Center; Bottom: Harper's Weekly*)

The Union monitor *Osage* was also designed and built by Eads and also weighed 523 tons. She was nearly identical to the *Neosho*, though she carried only two guns instead of four. Both vessels operated on the Red River under Porter. During the Red River Campaign, she ran aground on a sandbar and spent much of her time on the river stuck there. She was later sunk in Mobile Bay but raised. Sold to private interests after the war, she sank on Caddo Lake near Shreveport around 1870. *(Library of Congress)*

Lt. Cmdr. Thomas O. Selfridge Jr., was captain of the USS *Osage*. It was Selfridge who took possession of Alexandria, Louisiana, on behalf of the Union on March 16, 1864. Selfridge and engineer Tom Doughty built the first periscope in 1863 for looking over the turret of the *Osage*. Selfridge also commanded the experimental Union submarine *Alligator*. He eventually rose to the rank of Rear Admiral. *(Naval Historical Center)*

Shown above is the crew of the Federal ironclad gunboat *Choctaw* on the Red River during Porter's Expedition in April 1864. Their faces speak volumes. Note the extreme youth of some of the cabin boys. The sailor sixth from left in the front row has posed his dagger so that it is prominently in view. The sailor seventh from left, next to him, holds a cat, no doubt kept on board as a rat-control measure. *(Naval Historical Center)*

The tinclad USS *Ozark* was a monitor that operated on the Red River with Admiral Porter, who called her "a miserable vessel." Built in 1863, she had an Ericsson turret, but was never tested in serious action. *(Library of Congress)*

Pictured here are two views of the timberclad gunboat USS *Tyler*. Originally the sidewheel packet boat *A.O. Tyler*, she was sold to the U.S. government in June 1861 and rebuilt as a gunboat. She had a shallow draft and made a good reconnaissance vessel. *(Both photos: Naval Historical Center)*

The USS *Lexington* was sister to the *Tyler*. Built in 1858 as the sidewheeler *Victoria*, she was captured by the U.S. in 1862 and fitted out as an Ellet ram-type gunboat. She is seen here on the Red River as part of Admiral Porter's fleet. After the Civil War, she was sold into private hands. In 1868, she was damaged by a tornado at Vicksburg and shipped to the naval yards at Algiers, Louisiana, for repairs. There she burned on February 3, 1869. *(Library of Congress)*

Pictured here is the advance on Shreveport. Maj. Gen. Nathaniel P. Banks's army crosses the Red River 54 miles above Alexandria, Louisiana, just short of mid-way to the capital, on March 31, 1864. The Army of the Gulf under General Franklin is using both a traditional bridge and pontoons to cross. A supply train is seen at right. The Federals would make it to within 40 miles of Shreveport before being turned back at the Battle of Mansfield eight days later. (*Frank Leslie's Illustrated News*)

Retreating from Mansfield, Banks's army was once more routed at Pleasant Hill, Louisiana. On May 4, 1864, his army and Porter's fleet were again in Alexandria. The fanciful view above shows troops marching down Front Street as liberated slaves cheer. The actual scene was far less jubilant, and few civilians remained in the town. Later in May, as the army and navy retreated, they set the city afire. Below, part of Porter's fleet is shown at Alexandria on the Red. (*Top: Harper's Weekly; Bottom: Frank Leslie's Illustrated News*)

Above, the U.S. Naval Hospital vessel *Woodford* of the Mississippi Marine Brigade is pictured. She was wrecked crossing the falls above Alexandria and had to be burned. Below are transports of the Union fleet moored at Alexandria, just below the falls in April 1864. *(Top: LSU-Shreveport Noel Library Archives; Bottom: Naval Historical Center)*

These Union transport vessels at Alexandria, Louisiana, are waiting for the Red River's waters to rise in order to more easily cross the rapids located just above the city. In all, fifty-seven supply transports, two pump boats, five tug boats, one coal transport, one dispatch boat, and one hospital ship accompanied Porter's twenty-five gunboats up the Red River past Alexandria. (*Library of Congress*)

Above, the coal transport *William H. Brown* and the supply vessel *Benefit* are held by low water on the Red at Alexandria in May 1864. Below, the tinclad number 9, USS *Signal*, is seen at work building Bailey's Dam. The dam was designed by the engineer Col. Joseph Bailey to remedy the problem of low water on the river, so that the Union fleet could cross the rapids. As many as 3,000 men worked day and night to build the dam, allowing the Union fleet to retreat. The *Signal*, however, was among several boats captured by Confederates at Dunn's Bayou on May 5, 1864. *(Library of Congress)*

Although not altogether clear, the photograph above is an extraordinary image. It shows part of Admiral Porter's ironclad fleet above Alexandria, awaiting the completion of Bailey's Dam and the higher water that will take them over the rapids toward Alexandria in their retreat. The image was made sometime during the first days of May 1864 and shows, from left to right, the *Mound City*, two River City class gunboats (the *Carondelet*, *Louisville*, or *Pittsburg*), the coal transport *William H. Brown*, the supply vessel *Benefit*, the tug *Dahlia*, and the monitor *Neosho*. (*Naval Historical Center*)

Above is a rare image of Bailey's Dam, which raised the level of the Red River enough for the Union fleet to retreat downstream over the rapids that give Rapides Parish, Louisiana, its name. The hastily built dam included many hundreds of trees felled along the riverbank by Union troops, as well as much of the huge building of the Louisiana Seminary of Learning and Military Academy at Pineville (below), where Gen. William T. Sherman had been president before the outbreak of war. Few had faith that Colonel Bailey's concept would be successful, but by May 13, 1864, all the vessels of the fleet still afloat in Union hands had crossed safely, thanks to the dam. *(Top: Library of Congress; Bottom: Authors)*

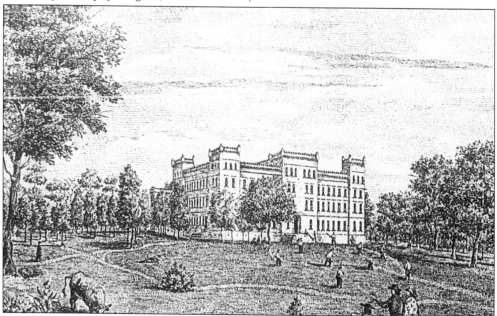

Pictured above, a contemporary engraving shows Admiral Porter's fleet passing through Bailey's Dam above Alexandria in May 1864. The scene is a fanciful Northern rendition. Few excited civilians would have been watching in reality. Furthermore, by then, the Federal forces had lost three transports, two gunboats, their hospital ship, and some 600 soldiers and sailors on the Red River itself (in addition to several thousand more in land engagements). Shown below is a more accurate rendition of the Union fleet crossing Bailey's Dam. (*Top: Frank Leslie's Illustrated News; Bottom: Harper's Weekly*)

A contemporary painting by James Alden shows the Union ironclad gunboats *Osage* and *Neosho* running through a break in Bailey's Dam to pass safely over the rapids in their retreat toward Alexandria on May 9, 1864. The view is from atop the dam, looking northwest. (*Naval Historical Center*)

During the Union advance on the Red, the quartermaster's boat *John Warner* ran aground and delayed the progress of the fleet. Shortly thereafter she was captured by the Confederates, who sank her across the channel in a fashion similar to the *New Falls City*, in order to halt the Union's retreat. In the above engraving, the Confederates are firing upon the *Warner* just prior to her capture. In the engraving below, the Confederates attack Union gunboats at Blair's Landing in an effort to run them aground and stop their retreat. In actuality, however, the retreat was only slightly delayed. (*Both photos: Frank Leslie's Illustrated News*)

The *Laurel Hill* was used by Admiral Porter as a transport vessel on the Red. In 1863, she briefly became an ocean-going vessel when she was sent by the Union Navy to Port Arthur, Texas, to silence some Confederate batteries. (*LSU-Shreveport Noel Library Archives*)

The *Black Hawk*, General Banks's command vessel, is not to be confused with Admiral Porter's flagship of the same name. Porter's *Black Hawk* was a tinclad gunboat (see page 40) while Banks's boat was a supply transport. She is seen here on the Red just after the Battle of Blair's Landing. Days after the Federal retreat, she was moored at New Orleans, where she caught fire on May 28, 1864. Eight boats moored near her caught fire also and were destroyed. (*Naval Historical Center*)

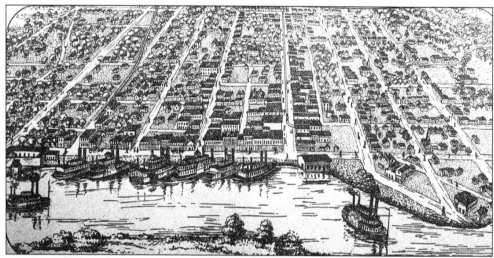

The Louisiana capital, Shreveport, is shown above as it appeared at the time of the Civil War. The city was spared attack by Union forces and came through the war unscathed. On May 26, 1865, the Trans-Mississippi Confederacy, with its headquarters at Shreveport, surrendered. It was the last major Confederate command to capitulate. Below is a view of Commerce Street on the Shreveport river-front at that time. The view is looking south from near Travis Street. (*Both photos: Authors*)

Pictured above is Lt. Charles W. Read of the Confederate Navy. Lieutenant Read, a veteran blockade-runner, made a last-ditch attempt to change the course of the Civil War in the Confederacy's favor by dashing from Shreveport down the Red River—now free of Union ships—toward the open sea. It was an attempt to reach the Gulf of Mexico and there harass Union shipping, hopefully turning the tide of the war. Although Read failed, it proved to be the last valiant Confederate naval effort in home waters against the Northern invaders. (*Authors*)

The CSS *William H. Webb* was a Confederate ironclad gunboat fitted out at Shreveport's Confederate Naval Yard. Together with the ironclad *Missouri* and the timber-clad *Merite* (also known both as the *Mary T.* and as the *J.A. Cotton*), it was all that remained of the Confederate flotilla at Shreveport by March 1865. It was the *Webb* that Read took on his dash to the sea. Accosted by Union gunboats at the mouth of the Red (some of the very boats which had served with Porter on the river months before), the *Webb* successfully outran and eluded them. Reaching New Orleans, she ran up a Union flag to masquerade as a Federal ship but was recognized. Ripping down the American flag, the Confederate banner was then defiantly raised. Besieged on all sides, the *Webb* was crippled by the U.S. Sloop of War *Richmond*, and set on fire by her own crew to prevent capture. It was the end of the Confederate Navy in Louisiana. *(Top: Painting by William L. Challoner, Collection of the Louisiana State Museum; Bottom: Harper's;)*

Three

THE RISE AND FALL OF POST-WAR STEAMBOAT COMMERCE

Contrary to common belief, the golden age of river steamboats came not during the antebellum period but after the end of the Civil War. The greatest period of trade on Southern waters occurred in the last three decades of the 19th century. It was also an era that saw the construction of the largest, grandest, and costliest boats ever to ply the waters of the Red River, the Mississippi River, or any of the Mississippi's other tributaries. Here, in an image probably made in the 1880s, a steamboat is being loaded with cargo. Passenger cabins were located on the upper decks. (*LSU-Shreveport Noel Library Archives*)

This is the sidewheel packet steamer *Richmond*. She is indicative of the great river steamboats of the era immediately following the Civil War. Indeed, the *Richmond* was built only a year after the war's end. Her life was very short, however. From 1866 to 1868, she operated on the Mississippi between New Orleans and St. Louis, Beginning in January 1868, she also ran between New Orleans and Shreveport. On December 3, 1869, she wrecked and sank at the hairpin turn just below Shreveport, known as Eagle Bend. Also lost at Eagle Bend was the *Kentucky*, which went down in flames with several hundred lives lost on June 9, 1865. The *Irene* sank at the same bend, only 23 days before the *Richmond*. The *Jimplecute* sank there a few years later. The site today is within the city of Shreveport, just south of Bickham Dickson Park, and near the campus of LSU-Shreveport. (*LSU-Shreveport Noel Library Archives*)

The mighty Anchor Line sidewheeler *City of Monroe*, seen here in two different views, was built in 1886. Most Anchor Line steamboats ran on the Mississippi and Tennessee Rivers, but the *City of Monroe* also ran on the Red and the Ouachita, on which the actual city of Monroe, Louisiana, is situated. Damaged in a tornado in 1896, she was rebuilt, but ended her days as an excursion vessel on the Mississippi during the St. Louis World's Fair. She burned near St. Louis on October 12, 1905. *(Both photos: Authors)*

Pictured above, the steamboat *LaBelle* was known as the "Dirty Belle" for the soot she emitted from her funnels. Built in 1869, she ran a regular route on the Mississippi and Red between New Orleans, Donaldsonville, and Shreveport. On February 8, 1878, she sank at Norman's Landing on the Red River, carrying 2,699 bales of cotton from Shreveport bound for market in New Orleans. Shown below is the *Peerless*, which is known to have been on the Red only a few times; she operated primarily on the Ohio, Arkansas, and Mississippi. She was built in 1865 and dismantled at Pensacola, Florida, in 1886. (*Top: Authors; Bottom: LSU-Shreveport Noel Library Archives*)

The most famous of all vessels to be found in the Red River's history is the *Robt. E. Lee*, built in 1869. On August 9, 1870, she arrived at Shreveport from New Orleans, the only record of her presence on the Red. Just five weeks earlier, she had won the famous race with the *Natchez* on the Mississippi between New Orleans and St. Louis. She was dismantled in 1876. The view above is marked "*Robt. E. Lee* at Shreveport" but the photograph may have actually been taken at New Orleans. The view below shows the interior of the *Lee*'s main saloon. (*Top: LSU-Shreveport Noel Library Archives; Bottom: Authors*)

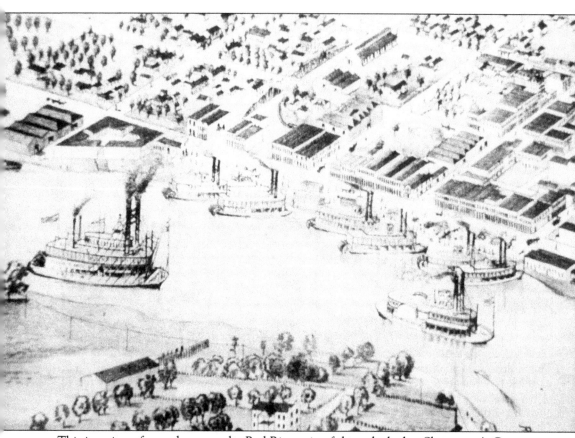

This is a view of steamboats on the Red River, six of them docked at Shreveport's Commerce Street wharf in 1872. The detail is from a lithograph entitled "Bird's Eye View of Shreveport," drawn by Herman Brossius with amazing accuracy. From left to right are the *John T. Moore, Little Fleur, Texas, Era No. 10, Belle Rowland,* an unidentified boat, the *Plaville,* and the *Henry M. Shreve.* The lithograph also shows three other steamboats not visible in this detail: the *Maria Louise,* the *Clifford,* and the ferry that operated between Shreveport and Bossier Parish across the Red. Three hundred lithographs of the "Bird's Eye View" were printed, but only a handful of originals survive; this image is from one of them. (*Authors*)

An indication of the vibrancy of late-19th-century river commerce is evident in the two images on this page. Above is a view of Shreveport's Commerce Street Wharf, or "Levee," *c.* 1890. Northwest Louisiana was then the richest cotton-growing region in the state and one of the richest in the South. Shreveport was its market center, and from there the cotton was shipped by steamboat to New Orleans (below) where Shreveport cotton is here seen being unloaded near the foot of Canal Street. The warehouse on the far right was owned by cotton factors Penick & Ford, a Shreveport Company with New Orleans offices. *(Top: Authors; Bottom: LSU-Shreveport Noel Library Archives)*

Above, five Mississippi-Red River packet boats are shown moored, probably at New Orleans, c. 1870. They are the *Continental, Ezra Powers, Mollie Able, Indiana,* and *General Quitman.* The *Mollie Able* ran a regular route between Shreveport and New Orleans throughout the 1870s. Below is part of the river-front at Shreveport in the 1890s. Seen here is the Strand Street wharf, or "Batture," near the mouth of Cross Bayou. Part of the Confederate Naval Yard had been located here during the Civil War. Clearly visible are the many cotton warehouses that lined the riverfront. The building with the tower was the massive Dreyfus Company warehouse. *(Top: LSU-Shreveport Noel Library Archives; Bottom: Authors)*

These are two more views of the Shreveport riverfront in the late 19th century. The engraving above gives a hint of the damage caused by the flood of May 1874, which sent the Red's waters over the wharves and into the city's business district. Such periodic floods were rare but not rare enough. Below is a view of the same area of the riverfront from a different angle, some 20 years later with the river at its normal level. The Texas Street Bridge crosses the Red at this point today. (*Top: Frank Leslie's Illustrated News; Bottom: Authors*)

Although somewhat blurred, this is an extremely rare image of the *Ruby*, wrecked on the bank of the Batture, at the mouth of Cross Bayou in Shreveport in August 1873. Her load of cattle, bound for New Orleans, drowned and their carcasses were blamed erroneously for the outbreak of yellow fever in Shreveport days later. The epidemic killed almost one-fifth of Shreveport's permanent population and caused the same number to flee the city permanently. Among those who perished was Lt. Eugene A. Woodruff, who is believed to have taken this photograph (see page 19). (*Authors*)

An earlier disaster involved the fiery wreck of the *Mittie Stephens* (see page 24). She sank on Caddo Lake near Swanson's Landing, Texas, en route from New Orleans to Jefferson, Texas, on February 12, 1869. Shown here is the cover of a composition commissioned by the master of the steamer several years earlier. It was played on deck to call passengers to dinner. *(Jesse DeWare, IV)*

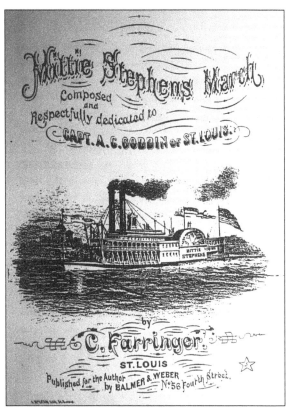

Cotton was both the lifeblood of the steamboat operators and their greatest hazard. Highly inflammable, it could turn an overloaded boat into an inferno very quickly. It was also highly absorbent and could take a boat to the bottom rapidly if waterlogged. The first Cooley Line boat named *Ouachita*, seen here carrying Ouachita Parish cotton to New Orleans c. 1899, was lucky, but many similarly overloaded boats were not. The *Ouachita* was in regular use until 1909 and was dismantled in 1914. *(Authors)*

This is a dramatic view of the sternwheel steamboat *Kate Woods*, loaded to her uppermost decks with Caddo and Bossier Parish cotton, headed for New Orleans. She is seen here on the Mississippi, having just passed into the great river from the Red. After the turn of the 20th century, such sights became more and more rare. (*Authors*)

Pictured above is the *Keokuk* at New Orleans in the 1880s. Built in 1876 as the *C.K. Peck*, she was renamed in 1882, making occasional trips between St. Louis and Shreveport between 1882 and 1884. After 1885, her service was limited to the New Orleans-Baton Rouge trade. Below is the Mississippi at St. Louis. The *Enterprise*, in the center foreground, operated on the Upper Mississippi from 1864 until 1868. She was then transferred to New Orleans, running between New Orleans and Shreveport regularly until 1871. *(Both photos: LSU-Shreveport Noel Library Archives)*

These two views are of one of the most famous Red River packet steamboats, the *Imperial*. She was built in 1894 for the Scovell brothers, steamboat operators, to carry cotton and passengers from Shreveport to New Orleans. The boat is seen below at the Canal Street wharf in New Orleans on March 28, 1895 preparing to unload her record cargo of 3,611 bales of Caddo and Bossier Parish cotton. *(Both photos: Authors)*

This is another picture of the *Imperial*. She was a grand boat but met a bizarre fate; she was eaten by shrimp—or at least her hull was. In February 1911, she made a trip from Monroe, Louisiana, to New Orleans where she was laid up in the shipyards at Algiers for repairs. While berthed there, shrimps bored into her oak hull and did irreparable damage, though this was not realized until swells from a passing tug sank her. On June 17, 1912, the portion above the water caught fire and burned, thus ending the illustrious career of the *Imperial*. (*Authors*)

Capt. Matthew LeGrand Scovell was a native of Ohio who grew up on the Ohio and Mississippi Rivers. His family operated numerous steamboats, eventually focusing their business almost entirely on the Red River, operating out of Shreveport. They produced five well-known pilots, including Matt, who was captain of the *Royal George*, *Joe Bryarly*, *Anna B. Adams*, *W.T. Scovell*, as well as the *Imperial*. (*Authors*)

The *C.E. Satterlee* is pictured here on the Red River in 1890. She was built in 1889 for the Texas and Pacific Railroad, to compete with the Red River line for the Shreveport-New Orleans trade. Her sister, the *E.B. Wheelock*, was built for the T. & P. at the same time and for the same purpose. The *C.E. Satterlee* sank at Rock River Bend on the Red River on October 29, 1893. The *Wheelock* was involved in a bizarre accident on July 23, 1890, when she signaled for the pivoting V.S. & P. Bridge at Shreveport to be opened. A passenger train signaled an instant later, but the bridge was already swinging wide. The wildly braking train did not quite make it, her locomotive and coal tender leaping into the river just ahead of the *Wheelock*. *(LSU-Shreveport Noel Library Archives)*

These two views of the C.E. Satterlee were both taken on the same day in 1891, as she lay moored at Shreveport's Lake Street wharf. In the photograph above, the E.B. Wheelock can be seen just to the left of the C.E. Satterlee. The E.B. Wheelock also sank on the Red, at Snaggy Point on May 3, 1895. In both photographs, the large house of Capt. S.J. Zieglar can be seen rising behind the C.E. Satterlee. In the photograph above, the one-story T.T. Land house, used by Gen. Edmund Kirby Smith as his residence during the Civil War, is visible just above the stern of the C.E. Satterlee. (Top: LSU-Shreveport Noel Library Archives; Bottom: Authors)

In 1935, John C. Gibbs, then 85, a veteran steamboatman of the Red and Mississippi Rivers, donned a suit he had kept since the 1860s and posed for a newspaper photographer. Gibbs first visited Shreveport just after the Civil War and spent much time in the city during his service on several Red River packet steamboats, particularly the *Kate Adams*. Gibbs eventually retired in New Orleans, recalling Shreveport as "a bustling border town" when first he visited there. The *Kate Adams*, renamed *Dewey* in 1898 and *Lotus Sims* in 1902, burned at St. Louis on October 28, 1903. (*Authors*)

A Red River packet boat is shown above, docked at the Bienville Street Wharf, New Orleans, in the 1870s. Below is an 1883 view of the wharf at Vicksburg, on the Mississippi. The Red River cotton packet *LeFlore* is prominent in the foreground. She also ran on the Yazoo and Ohio Rivers. *(Both photos: LSU-Shreveport Noel Library Archives)*

This is the *Valley Queen*, a Shreveport-New Orleans cotton packet steamer. In her day, she carried many thousands of bales of north Louisiana cotton to market in New Orleans. She burned on the Mississippi near St. Joseph, Louisiana, while loaded with cotton and cottonseed in March 1903. (*Authors*)

The *Hallette*, a Red River Line steamboat, was one of two named for the daughters of Shreveport cotton planter and banker Howard Clinton Stringfellow. The other was the *Garland* (see page 105). The two views on this page both show the *Hallette* laden with Caddo Parish cotton, much of it, no doubt, from Stringfellow's plantation. Built in 1887, she ran until 1906. *(Both photos: Authors)*

The *Belle*, pictured here, was probably photographed on Bayou LaFourche in 1880. Built in 1875, she ran a regular route on the Mississippi and Red Rivers between New Orleans and Shreveport beginning in 1878. Her career continued into the 1880s. *(LSU-Shreveport Noel Library Archives)*

Shreveport's Commerce Street wharf, or "Levee," is seen here from the Lower Water Street wharf in 1872. The barrels contain cargo shipped in from New Orleans. Plows can be seen at right foreground, and a planter, at left, discusses the cargo with workmen. From Shreveport's docks, much cotton left for New Orleans. In exchange, New Orleans packets brought goods of every description to the bustling marketplaces of Shreveport and Alexandria. (*Frank Leslie's Illustrated News*)

This is an image of the *Betsy Ann*, a cotton and cargo packet that saw service on many American rivers including the Pennsylvania, Ohio, Mississippi, Red, and numerous bayous. She is seen here on a bayou sometime in the 1910s. Known for speed, she ran several races as late as the 1920s before being put to use as a towboat. She was dismantled in 1940. (*LSU-Shreveport Noel Library Archives*)

Pictured here is Capt. Mary Miller. On February 18, 1884, Captain Miller became the first woman licensed to pilot steamboats on the Red, Ouachita, and Mississippi Rivers. She was the wife of Capt. George "Old Natural" Miller, a veteran steamboat master whose career began just prior to the start of the Civil War. (*Authors*)

Capt. W.F. Dillon, an important Red River steamboat master, was born in Ohio and grew up on the Ohio River near Ironton, where he learned the steamboat trade from the ground up. He was a crew member of many Ohio and Mississippi riverboats and was captain of numerous Red River and Mississippi packets, including the *Ashland, Bonnie Lee, John D. Scully, Friendly, Nat. F. Dortch, New Haven,* and *Rosa Bland.* He was an executive with the Red River Line, and was later president of both Shreveport's First National Bank and the city's streetcar system. (*Authors*)

The connections between the significant Red River ports of Shreveport and Alexandria, and the port of New Orleans (once the largest cargo port in all of North America), were strong and very significant. Goods from New Orleans went to the interior of Louisiana, Texas, and the Indian Territory (Oklahoma) via the packets that operated on the Red River. Cotton, beef and dairy cattle, and various fruits and cereals went to New Orleans from these same points. Several of these Red River Packets at New Orleans are pictured above in 1870. Below is the Red River Pilots' Association's communal tomb at New Orleans' Masonic Cemetery, built in 1869 and used through to the 1890s. (*Top: Authors; Bottom: photograph by Eric J. Brock, 1994*)

Shown above is the the *Era No. 10*, the tenth of 13 packet boats named *Era*. She was operated by the Kouns Line between Shreveport and New Orleans (see also pages 26 and 76). The *Era No. 10* was one of the most important Red River cotton packets of her day. Built in 1868, she survived several wrecks and remained in operation until destroyed by fire in 1892. *(Authors)*

Shown above, the *Columbia*, built in 1893, ran the New Orleans-Shreveport trade for the Carter Packet Company. She was sold in 1901 and ended her days as a showboat's towing vessel. She wrecked on the Ohio River on March 25, 1908. Below is the *Henry Frank*, built in 1878; it was one of the most important cotton carriers on the Mississippi and Red Rivers. On October 2, 1884, she caught fire 22 miles above New Orleans and was lost. *(Both photos: Authors)*

This is an engraving of the *Henry Frank* as she appeared at the port of New Orleans on April 2, 1881, loaded with 9,226 bales of cotton. It was the largest single cargo of cotton carried on any steamboat on any American river, before or since. (*Frank Leslie's Illustrated News*)

oseph LaBarge, Master.
rst boat to ascend
ssouri River to
. Benton.

The *DeSmet* carried materials to Shreveport for the building of the Southern Pacific Railroad in Louisiana and Arkansas. She later became the first steamboat to ascend the Missouri River to Ft. Benton, Montana. She later ran on the Missouri, Ohio, and Mississippi Rivers. She burned at Newport, Arkansas on June 12, 1886. *(LSU-Shreveport Noel Library Archives)*

The important Cooley Line cotton packet *America*, was built in 1898 for the New Orleans to Monroe, Louisiana trade. She ran primarily on the Mississippi, Ouachita, and Red Rivers. The *America* was one of the last big cotton packets to remain in operation. Seen here in her early and halcyon days, she later was used to ship such diverse cargoes as Budweiser Beer (from St. Louis to New Orleans), automobiles, and sporting goods. Seen here, she is being loaded with cottonseed in 1899. *(Authors)*

Capt. LeVerrier Cooley of the Cooley Line is at the wheel of the *America* in October 1907. When he died in 1931, the bell of the *America* was placed on top of his grave in New Orleans' Metairie Cemetery, where it remains today as his monument. Captain Cooley piloted a dozen steamboats during his career. *(LSU-Shreveport Noel Library Archives)*

These are two further views of the *America*, both while docked at New Orleans. In January 1924, she was chartered for the making of the movie *Magnolia*, in which she appears as the *Winnfield Scott*. She wrecked at the dock at the foot of Walnut Street in New Orleans on August 13, 1926, and was dismantled. *(Both photos: LSU-Shreveport Noel Library Archives)*

The sternwheeler *Red River* was built in 1899 for the Red River Packet Company. She is seen above, at the foot of Texas Street in Shreveport *c.* 1900. Below, the *Red River* is at Shreveport's Lower Water Street wharf, at about the same period. The Vicksburg, Shreveport, and Pacific Railroad Bridge, built in 1884, can be seen in the background. *(Both photos: Authors)*

Pictured here is the *City of Shreveport,* a late sternwheel packet steamboat. She ran on the Red, Ouachita, Black, and Mississippi Rivers from 1909 until 1921, when she burned near Monroe. (*LSU-Shreveport Noel Library Archives*)

LaFourche was a New Orleans-based packet steamboat that was built in 1888. She is seen here docked at New Orleans *c.* 1905; the spire of St. Louis Cathedral can be clearly seen in the background at far right. This was the second steamer to be named *LaFourche*, for the Louisiana bayou of the same name. The first was built in 1859 and dismantled in 1869. The second, shown above, burned at Twelve Mile Point, Louisiana, on September 20, 1907. *(Authors)*

The Red River Line's *Garland*, built in 1887, was named for Garland Stringfellow of Shreveport. Her sister boat, the *Hallette*, was also named for a Stringfellow daughter (see page 91). The *Garland* is seen here at New Orleans c. 1890; she sank in 1893. Note the famous *Natchez* to the left of the *Garland*. *(Authors)*

Above is a picture of the Red River Line's *Electra*, leaving Knox Point on the Red River in 1898. This is an exceptional image, as it clearly shows the churning of the water by the ship's huge paddlewheel. The *Electra* was built in 1897 and re-named *Sunny South* in 1914. She capsized in Mobile Bay in 1917. Below is the *Concordia*, built in 1906. She ran on the Mississippi, Red, Ouachita, and Black Rivers. She sank in 1913 with a dozen deaths and was raised a year later. Rebuilt, she operated as the *Uncle Oliver*, and was dismantled in 1924. *(Both photos: Authors)*

Small, steam-powered craft were used locally in most river cities. Above, the ferry *C.R. Watkins* is shown on the Red at Shreveport, *c.* 1890. Below, sand is being dredged from the Red River's bottom in order to make cement. Many older buildings of Shreveport, Alexandria, and smaller communities on the Red employ mortar made from river sand. The small workboat in this *c.* 1900 photograph belonged to the Chatwin Brothers, cement manufacturers of Shreveport. Some of the cottonseed oil mills at East Shreveport, today known as Bossier City, can be seen in the background. *(Both photos: Authors)*

The *D.L. Tally*, named for Shreveport businessman Dew Lafayette Tally, is pictured above. She was built in 1870 and operated on the Red and Mississippi between Shreveport and New Orleans until 1873, when she was sold and transferred to Mobile, Alabama. She burned at Mobile on March 29, 1895. (*Authors*)

Monroe, Louisiana, is shown above in the 1890s. What Shreveport was to the Red, Monroe was to the Ouachita—the river's most important port. Founded in 1785 as Ft. Miro, it was renamed in 1819 in honor of the *James Monroe,* the first steamboat to successfully ascend the Ouachita to reach that point. This view is of the intersection of DeSiard and South Grand Streets, close to the waterfront, looking east. Below is the Ouachita, Red, and Mississippi packet boat *D'Arbonne,* docked at New Orleans *c.* 1885. She was photographed by the noted New Orleans photographer G.F. Mugnier. *(Both photos: Authors)*

The *Wm. Garig* was built in 1904 for the New Orleans-Monroe trade. She operated as such on the Mississippi, Black, Ouachita, and Red Rivers until 1918, when she was renamed the *Golden Eagle*. In 1932, she ceased being a packet boat and became a tourist vessel on the Tennessee, Ohio, Cumberland, and Mississippi Rivers. As a pleasure vessel, she was in competition with the *Delta Queen* (built 1926) until May 17, 1947, when she sank on the Mississippi. She is seen here on the Black River in Louisiana, October 1912. *(LSU-Shreveport Noel Library Archives)*

The *G.W. Sentell* was built in 1882 as the *Henry A. Tyler*, but was renamed for a Bossier Parish, Louisiana, planter in 1890, after her purchase by Bulow W. Marston of Shreveport. She operated between New Orleans and Jefferson, Texas, via the Red River to Shreveport, then through Twelve Mile Bayou and Caddo Lake to Jefferson, where this photograph was made in 1891. She burned near New Orleans, on December 28, 1894. (*LSU-Shreveport Noel Library Archives*)

Above is the *Colonel A.P. Kouns*, also docked at Jefferson. She followed the same regular route as the *G.W. Sentell*. Owned by the Kouns Line of Shreveport, she was built in 1874. On April 12, 1878, she sank on the Red, 70 miles above its mouth. Below is the *Lillie M. Barlow* at Jefferson, Texas, in August 1900. Built that same year, she operated between New Orleans and Jefferson, via Shreveport. She was the last regular packet boat to visit Jefferson in 1903, the year she sank at Derry's Landing, Louisiana. *(Top: Authors; Bottom: LSU-Shreveport Noel Library Archives)*

William Jennings Bryan arrives in Shreveport during the presidential campaign of 1900. Bryan did much of his campaign traveling via riverboat. Here, his campaign boat is docking at the Commerce Street wharf, having just passed through the Vicksburg, Shreveport, and Pacific Railroad Bridge, which can be seen in the background. Bryan was accompanied from his vessel by Shreveport's mayor, Ben Holzman, up Texas Street to the Caddo Parish Courthouse, where he gave a lengthy and well-attended speech (political events were then a form of public entertainment). He then left town, again aboard his boat. Note the cameraman at right. This photograph was taken by Miss Flavia Van Lear, later Leary. (*Authors*)

The showboats named *New Sensation* (there were five of them) floated on the Red River, as well as on the Mississippi and her other major tributaries, between 1878 and 1900. Built and operated by Capt. Augustus Byron French, the *New Sensation*, like almost all showboats, was essentially a barge upon which a theater was constructed. This was towed or, more generally, pushed, by a tugboat from town to town along the rivers. The engravings on this page are of the interior and exterior of the *New Sensation No. 2*, which was seen on the Red many times. (*Both images: Authors*)

The showboat *New Sunny South*, which belonged to W.R. Markle, is shown above being pushed up the Red, shortly after her construction in 1905. Many other showboats ran on the Red as late as the 1920s. Today's riverboat casinos, seen in Shreveport and Bossier City, are the successors to the showboats of old; modified and enclosed barges resembling traditional steamboats. In the cases of the modern casino boats, they are not towed or pushed, but operate on diesel power, which is the only essential difference from their showboat predecessors. Below are the workboats *Jas. L. Hale* and *Katherine Hale* on the east bank of the Red, opposite Shreveport, c. 1900. Casino boats today are moored along the same banks. *(Both photos: Authors)*

The U.S. government snagboat *C.W. Howell* is seen above, during the clean-up following the flood of May 1890. The location is the Lower Water Street wharf area of Shreveport, which was closed shortly after another destructive flood in 1905. The location is today part of the linear park, fronting the Red River along the Clyde Fant Memorial Parkway (named for a longtime 20th-century mayor of the city). The area was frequently inundated by the rising river in the 19th and early 20th centuries. A view of this same location during a flood can be seen on page 79. Another view of this same site, during its most active period, can be found on page 93. (*Authors*)

The *C.W. Howell* is depicted at Shreveport in these two views. She is pictured at the foot of Texas Street, along the Commerce Street wharf, *c.* 1885. The 305-ton *C.W. Howell* was built in St. Louis in 1881. Both photographs on this page were made on the same day. In the upper image, the pivoting center section of the Vicksburg, Shreveport, and Pacific Railroad Bridge can be seen swung open. Workboats are evident in both photographs, including the tugboat *Advance,* which is pushing a barge upriver in the photograph below. *(Both photos: LSU-Shreveport Noel Library Archives)*

This was the end of the *C.W. Howell*. During the flood of 1905, she struck a pier of the Vicksburg, Shreveport, and Pacific Railroad Bridge at Shreveport and foundered. The *Howell* is especially significant since she was the longest operating of the 15 government snagboats to patrol the Red during the 19th century. (*LSU-Shreveport Noel Library Archives*)

Construction on the Cotton Belt Bridge across the Red River at Shreveport took place in 1915. Located just downstream from the Vicksburg, Shreveport, and Pacific Bridge, the Cotton Belt Bridge opened in 1917. In the 20th century, other bridges were built across the Red at numerous points. Many were railroad bridges, indicators of the coming dominance of the railroad over the riverboat as the region's principal means of transportation. *(LSU-Shreveport Noel Library Archives)*

A locomotive of the Vicksburg, Shreveport, and Pacific Railroad crosses the V.S. & P.'s bridge over the Red River between Shreveport and Bossier City in 1903. By the time this photograph was taken, the railroad had emerged as the unquestionably preeminent means of transportation in the South, a distinction it had long since achieved elsewhere in the United States. *(Authors)*

The sternwheel steamboat *Amy Hewes*, seen here c. 1905 on Bayou Teche, was typical of small riverboats of the late nineteenth century, many of which were still operating early in the 20th century. Such boats carried passengers, cargo, and mail from the major rivers such as the Red, Atchafalaya, and Mississippi, through the bayous and swamps of south and central Louisiana, providing an important link to the rest of the state for the areas they served. (*Authors*)

In 1916, the Vicksburg, Shreveport, and Pacific Bridge was acquired by the Illinois Central Gulf Railroad, which partially rebuilt it. The bridge is today owned by the Kansas City Southern Railroad and still can be opened for riverboat traffic. The view above is of the Horseshoe Casino's riverboat *King of the Red*, as seen from the bridge today. The photograph on the left shows the bridge's central turning mechanism, which allows the central span to swing open for passing boats, just as it has done since 1884. (*Photos by Eric J. Brock, March 1999*)

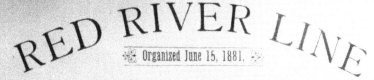

In this 1882 advertisement for the Red River Line, the cooperation between the riverboats and the railroads is evident, though the railroads were already beginning to supplant the riverboats. In 1883, the value of goods shipped by rail to and from Shreveport was equal to that shipped by steamboat. By 1886, the railroads were handling six times as much cargo. By 1910, the amount of cargo handled by riverboats on the Red was insignificant. (*Authors*)

The *General John Newton* (above), was a government inspection boat that was operated on the Red and Mississippi Rivers by the Army Corps of Engineers from 1899 to 1957. It is seen here on the Red, *c.* 1915. She is owned today by the University of Minnesota. Below are two sternwheel steamboats, their identification uncertain but probably owned by the Texas and Pacific Railroad. They are docked at Shreveport's Lake Street wharf, which was owned by the T.&P. in the 1890s. In the background is the V.S.&P. Bridge. By the 1890s, river packets were often owned by the railroads, minimizing the cut-throat competition. *(Top: LSU-Shreveport Noel Library Archives; Bottom: Authors)*

Shown above, the *River Rose* was the first commercial paddlewheeler to operate on the Red River in the second half of the 20th century. Christened in 1984, the small excursion boat operated a regular route between Shreveport and Bossier City until 1988. She now operates on the Ohio River at Cincinnati. Below is the enormous sternwheel of the *Queen of the Red*, which was moored at the Port of Shreveport-Bossier, south of Shreveport, in March 1999. The *Queen of the Red* and the *King of the Red* are both owned by Horseshoe Casino, one of the five casino companies operating boats on the Red River today. (Top photo by Neil Johnson; bottom photo by Eric J. Brock)

The *Rose of Shreveport,* owned by Harrah's Casino, was brought upriver to Shreveport in 1993. Seen here on her arrival day, she was only the second commercial paddlewheel vessel to navigate the upper Red River since the 1920s. As of this writing (1999), six riverboat casinos have been brought to Shreveport and Bossier City, the largest being Horseshoe Casino's *King of the Red,* the longest vessel ever seen on the river, save for barges. Although the riverboat casinos are paddlewheel vessels that resemble the steamboats of old, they are, in reality, much more similar to the showboats that once operated on the river. The showboats were pushed or towed by other craft, however, while the riverboat casinos are diesel-powered. Their layout and purpose, however, is decidedly similar. *(Photograph by Nan Weaver)*

Because of the many sinkings of steamboats on the Red River, and because of the numerous wrecked and abandoned riverboats found along her banks, the Red came to be known as the "steamboat graveyard" in the late 19th century. The decline and final cessation of riverboat travel early in the 20th century made the tragic nickname even more poignant. Hundreds of vessels plied the Red during the golden century of steamboat travel. Dozens of these ships wrecked, burned, or sank, and literally thousands of lives were lost, yet the steamboat era remains an epoch filled with romantic fascination even to the present day. This engraving, entitled "Steamboat Graveyard," which appeared in *Harper's Weekly* on September 15, 1888, speaks volumes.

In 1962, the United States issued a postage stamp commemorating the sesquicentennial of Louisiana's statehood. For its design, a Red River to Mississippi River packet steamboat of the mid-19th century was chosen. It was a fitting choice, for few entities had so great an impact on Louisiana's development during that era as did the river steamboat.

Acknowledgments

The authors wish to extend their thanks to all those who have provided support, materials, photos, and information for this book: Archivist Laura Street and the staff of the Louisiana State University at Shreveport Noel Memorial Library Department of Archives and Special Collections, the staff of the Naval Historical Center at the Washington Navy Yard, the Library of Congress, DeAnne Blanton of the National Archives and Records Administration, the Howard-Tilton Memorial Library at Tulane University, John House at the Mansfield (Louisiana) State Commemorative Area, Duke Rivet of the Louisiana State Division of Archaeology, Archaeologist Tad Britt of the U.S. Army Corps of Engineers (Vicksburg District), Erwin Roemer of the U.S. Army Corps of Engineers (Memphis District), Charles Pearson of Coastal Environments, Inc., of Baton Rouge, Steve James of PanAmerican Consulting of Memphis, and the staff of R. Christopher Goodwin and Associates of Frederick, Maryland.

The Authors

Eric Brock is a well-known Louisiana historian. He is a columnist for the *Shreveport Journal's* editorial page and has published several books on Shreveport and New Orleans history. He is a lifelong resident of Shreveport, Louisiana, and a graduate of Centenary College of Louisiana.

Gary Joiner is a professor of history at Louisiana State University in Shreveport. He is also a professional cartographer and is the author of numerous published articles. He is a native of Farmerville, Louisiana, and a graduate of Louisiana Tech University.

Visit us at
arcadiapublishing.com

Printed in the USA
CPSIA information can be obtained
at www.ICGtesting.com
LVHW010016021123
762837LV00007B/96